A
New
PORCINE HISTORY
of PHILOSOPHY
and RELIGION

James C. Taylor

ABINGDON PRESS / Nashville

A NEW PORCINE HISTORY OF PHILOSOPHY AND RELIGION

Copyright © 1972, 1992 by Abingdon Press

Library of Congress Cataloging-in-Publication Data

Taylor, James C., 1934–
   A new porcine history of philosophy and religion. / James C. Taylor.
   p. cm.

   ISBN 0-687-27866-X (alk. paper)
   1. Philosophy-Caricatures and cartoons.   2. Religion-Caricatures and cartoons.   3. American wit and humor, Pictorial   I. Title.
NC1429.T34A4   1992   92-2621
741.5′973–dc20   CIP

Printed in the United States of America
on recycled, acid-free paper

Preface

It's been about two decades now since I happened to have a scratchpad in front of me while I was listening to one of my colleagues in a team-taught course lecturing on some problem in axiology. My interest in drawing and my enjoyment of philosophy and theology were suddenly united, and the first of the philosophical pigs saw the light of day.

As I pointed out in the original version of the book, the combination is quite natural. First, pigs are the wisest of all the farm animals, even as philosophers and theologians are (according to ancient tradition, at least, if not by modern evidence) the wisest of people. Second, theology is the most enjoyable of all human endeavors (with philosophy—one would hope—not too poor a second); since pigs have a greater capacity for enjoyment than any other animal, it follows that there must be something theologian-like in every pig (leaving for another time any debate over the corollary). Third, and most important, I find pigs easier to draw than most other animals.

The world of pigs has not changed much since the first edition was published. Pigs, it appears, have pretty well arrived at the stage of development they consider themselves to have been intended for, and there's not much reason for them to change. I'll save my assessment of the theologians and philosophers till I figure out how to read the stuff they are writing these days. Meanwhile it's probably best to let the cartoons speak for themselves.

A good deal of inspiration and quite a number of specific suggestions were provided by my colleagues in that teaching team—Mr. Leo Wernke, Mr. William Landram, and Dr. Ann Marie

Shannon. Others, notably my old friends Douglas and Mary Mc-Pherson and my patient wife, Helen, also made suggestions and provided helpful criticisms. The best features of the original book were the result of what all these gracious and friendly people contributed, and I want to thank them again. I'd also like to thank Bob Ratcliff and the other folks at Abingdon who decided to publish this new edition, offered several specific suggestions for new cartoons, and provided valuable help in revising it and bringing it up to date.

I dedicated the first edition to my children, Janet and Peter. They are twenty years older now than they were then, and have reputations to worry about, but I'm going to repeat the dedication anyway.

Jefferson, Oklahoma
November, 1991

CONTENTS

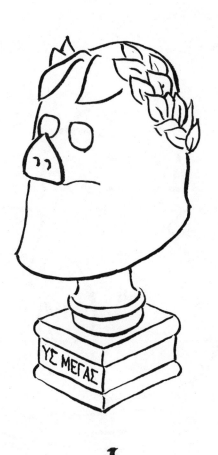

I

CLASSIC GREEK PIGS

STOIC PIG

EPICUREAN PIG

SIMPLISTIC HEDONIST PIG RISING
ON A MORNING AFTER, TO SERVE
AS AN OBJECT LESSON TO MORE
MODERATE PIGS EVERYWHERE

ANTI-HERACLITEAN PIG
ATTEMPTING TO STEP INTO
THE SAME STREAM TWICE

SOCRATIC PIG AND YOUTHFUL DISCIPLE IN DIALOGUE

ARISTOTELIAN PIG CONTEMPLATING ACORN

PLATONIC
PHILOSOPHER KING

II

PIGS OF THE ANCIENT AND MEDIEVAL CHURCH

AUGUSTINIAN PIGS SINNING BECAUSE OF THEIR FALLEN NATURE

PELAGIAN PIGS SINNING JUST
BECAUSE THEY WANT TO

BOETHIAN PIG BEING CONSOLED
BY PHILOSOPHY

REALIST PIG AND NOMINALIST PIG CONSIDERING EAR OF CORN

OCKHAMIST PIG
PONDERING MEANS
OF EXAMINING
PHILOSOPHICAL ASSERTIONS

ABELARDIAN PIG RESOLVING A
YES AND NO QUESTION

FRANCISCAN PIG AND CONGREGATION

III
Protestant Pigs

CALVINIST PIG BEING
SAVED BECAUSE HE IS
PREDESTINED TO BE
AMONG THE ELECT

ARMINIAN PIG BEING
SAVED BECAUSE HE FREELY
ACCEPTED THE GRACE
OF GOD

LUTHERAN PIG DEALING WITH ADVERSARY

ANGLICAN PIG GLORYING IN
ONE OF THE MORE PROVOCATIVE
PASSAGES OF HOOKER'S *LAWS
OF ECCLESIASTICAL POLITY*

ANGLICAN PIG FOLLOWING THE
VIA MEDIA

PURITAN PIG STRIVING TO MAKE HIS ELECTION SURE

METHODIST PIG WHOSE HEART
HAS BEEN STRANGELY WARMED

LITTLE BAND OF METHODIST
PIGS FLEEING FROM THE WRATH
TO COME

UNITED METHODISTS AREN'T HINDUS! (AT LEAST MOST OF THEM AREN'T)

UNITED METHODIST PIG GOING OUT
TO EXPLAIN TO THE WORLD WHAT
THE WORD "UNITED" SIGNIFIES

CAMPBELLITE PIG BEING SILENT WHERE THE BIBLE IS SILENT

SOUTHERN BAPTIST PIG

SOUTHERN BAPTIST PIGS RECEIVING LATEST UPDATE ON WHAT THEY BELIEVE ABOUT THE SCRIPTURES

MISSOURI SYNOD LUTHERAN PIG
CAUGHT UP IN THE HEAT OF
ECUMENICAL FERVOR

IV

Modern Philosophical Pigs

LEIBNIZIAN PIG PONDERING THE
DESIGN OF THE UNIVERSE

HUMEAN PIG DEVELOPING A
CRITICISM OF THE ARGUMENT
FROM DESIGN

NOVICE CARTESIAN PIG TRYING
TO FIGURE OUT WHERE HE WENT
WRONG

BERKELEIAN PIG NOT BEING PERCEIVED

ROUSSEAUEAN PIG
ENCOUNTERING A NOBLE SAVAGE

KANTIAN PIG PRIOR TO AWAKENING FROM HIS DOGMATIC SLUMBERS

KANTIAN PIG REFUSING TO LIE
TO A MANIAC WHO HAS ASKED
THE WHEREABOUTS OF HIS FRIEND

HEGELIAN PIG OBSERVING A
THETICAL PIG AND AN ANTITHETICAL
PIG ARRIVING AT A SYNTHESIS

KIERKEGAARDIAN PIG
DEMONSTRATING A LEAP OF FAITH

V

TWENTIETH CENTURY PIGS

NIETZSCHEAN SUPERPIG

EXISTENTIALIST PIG WITH AN ACUTE CASE OF ANGST

BERGSONIAN PIG ABOUT TO HAVE
AN IDEA WHICH NEVER EXISTED
BEFORE

BARTHIAN PIG

TILLICHIAN PIG BECOMING FRUSTRATED IN HIS EFFORTS TO DETERMINE WHICH OF HIS CONCERNS IS ULTIMATE

BONHOFFERIAN AND SARTRIAN
PIGS ARGUING OVER WHETHER WHAT
THEIR COMPANION HAS JUST DONE
AROSE FROM CHEAP GRACE OR
BAD FAITH

LOGICAL POSITIVIST PIG
DEVELOPING AN INFORMAL LIST
OF EMOTIVE TERMS

NIEBUHRIAN PIG ATTEMPTING
TO REALIZE LOVE AND JUSTICE
IN A CONTINUOUS DIALECTIC

ORDINARY LANGUAGE PIG
DOING RESEARCH

SITUATION ETHICS PIG AND
PRINCIPLES ETHICS PIG DISCUSSING
THE NATURE OF CHRISTIAN LOVE

WOEFULLY INEXPERIENCED
GROUP OF LIBERATIONIST PIGS
WHO HAVE JUST ESTABLISHED A
BASS COMMUNITY AND NOW ARE
WONDERING WHAT TO DO NEXT.

LIBERATION PIG TRYING TO
FIGURE OUT WHY IT'S SO MUCH
EASIER TO TALK WITH HIS
FRIEND THE CATHOLIC PIG THAN
WITH CERTAIN OTHER PIGS IN HIS
OWN MAINLINE DENOMINATION

EVANGELICAL PIG TRYING TO
FIGURE OUT WHY IT'S SO MUCH
EASIER TO TALK WITH HIS
FRIEND THE BAPTIST PIG THAN
WITH CERTAIN OTHER PIGS IN HIS
OWN MAINLINE DENOMINATION

POSTMODERNIST PIG
TRYING TO FIGURE OUT
WHY IT'S SO HARD TO TALK
WITH ANYBODY AT ALL

DECONSTRUCTIONIST PIG
INTERPRETING A TEXT

PIG WHO HAS FOUND
ALL THE ANSWERS

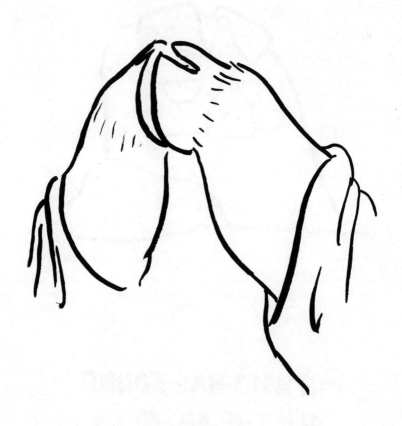